IMAGES
of America

THEATRES OF
SAN JOSE

CALIFORNIA THEATRE

Saturday Evening, May 31,

POSITITIVELY LAST APPEARANCE

Of the popular comedian,

MR. JOSEPH MURPHY!

— AND A —

FIRST CLASS COMPANY,

——On which occasion——

SHAUN RHUA,

A New and Original Irish Drama, written expressly for Mr. MURPHY,
will be presented for the first time in California.

CAST OF CHARACTERS:

Larry Donavan...............Mr. Joseph Murphy
Gerald Kavanagh.....................................Mr. Frank G. Cotter
Morris Donavan.......................................Mr. John Woodard
Bryan Calaghan.......................................Mr. John S. Lindsay
Patrick Kavanagh.....................................Mr. H. M. Brown
Lawyer Waddy..Mr. W. C. Lawrence
Peter Calaghan.......................................Mr. George L. Stevens
Wm. Sommetville....................................Mr. Louis Belmore
Hugh Burke..Mr. Geo. Bowman
Teddy Phats...Mr. E. Drum
Kate Donavan......................................Miss Georgie Woodthorpe
Dora Kavanagh ....Miss Kitty Belmore
Tim...Miss Lotta Chissold

[TOWN TALK EXTRA.]

San Jose's first of three theatres to bear the name "California" opened in 1879 in the former Central Hall building, located at 85 South Second Street. As with so many early theatres, it was destroyed by fire. In 1892, a youth tossed a cigarette into a firework stand, igniting a conflagration that burned the theatre and several adjacent buildings. (History San Jose.)

ON THE COVER: Well-attired San Joseans crowd Market Street in front of the Liberty Theatre around 1916. A screen adaptation of Hall Cane's novel *The Bondman*, starring William Farnum, is the attraction. The Liberty, with its marquee canopy of stained glass, opened in 1914 and was designed by San Jose architects William Binder and Ernest N. Curtis. (John C. Gordon Collection; Special Collections and Archives, San Jose State University.)

IMAGES
of America

THEATRES OF
SAN JOSE

Gary Lee Parks

ARCADIA
PUBLISHING

Copyright © 2009 by Gary Lee Parks
ISBN 978-0-7385-6906-2

Published by Arcadia Publishing
Charleston SC, Chicago IL, Portsmouth NH, San Francisco CA

Printed in the United States of America

Library of Congress Control Number: 2008942608

For all general information contact Arcadia Publishing at:
Telephone 843-853-2070
Fax 843-853-0044
E-mail sales@arcadiapublishing.com
For customer service and orders:
Toll-Free 1-888-313-2665

Visit us on the Internet at www.arcadiapublishing.com

To Edwin R. Parks (1915–1999), animator for Disney
and Hanna-Barbera Studios, among others.
A gifted artist, a supreme storyteller, and a terrific dad.

CONTENTS

ACKNOWLEDGMENTS

My thanks go to John Bondi, who first introduced me to San Jose's theatrical past. To the following individuals and organizations, for furnishing photographs and information, I am grateful: Steve Levin, personal collection; Jack Tillmany, personal collection; Jim Reed, History San Jose; Danelle Moon, Special Collections and Archives, San Jose State University; Johan Koning, Sunnyvale Historical Society and Museum Association; Paul Kopach, Los Gatos Public Library; Jim Narveson, the City of Santa Clara History Collection, the Santa Clara Art and History Consortium; Chuck Schoppe, Saratoga Historical Foundation; Theatre Historical Society of America; Chuck Bergtold; Tom DeLay; Steve Kaplowitz; Shirlie Montgomery; Martin Schmidt; Carol Jensen, for putting me in touch with Arcadia Publishing; Kelly Reed, my editor, for her enthusiastic guidance; my wife, Rebecca June Parks, for proofreading and for sharing the love of knowledge for knowledge's sake; and my mom, Leah Parks, for always prodding me to "Write something!"

INTRODUCTION

San Jose was the first secular Spanish settlement in California, first state capital, cultural and administrative hub of the agricultural Eden known as the Valley of Heart's Delight, and finally, the capital of Silicon Valley. Every large city has its own rich history, and part of that story is the way in which a hard-working public spends its leisure time. San Jose holds just such a record of its early entertainment history. Chief among this record are the theatre buildings that were constructed in San Jose's growing downtown, its neighborhoods, and the smaller cities and towns immediately surrounding it.

Imagine the owner of a Santa Clara Valley farm heading into San Jose with his wife and children for a night of vaudeville acts. Envision a laborer from the same farm, after having spent his week in the sun-drenched orchards, seeking an hour's respite in a little motion picture theatre in Campbell where, for a nickel's admission, he could laugh at the antics of comedians on-screen or perhaps view a short travelogue of images from lands he would never visit.

A decade or two later, as San Jose continued growing, the children of the next generation would be able to have an exciting night on the town, driving up and down neon-illuminated streets, where scintillating marquees heralded the latest movie offerings from Hollywood. Perhaps they would instead choose to venture out from downtown to one of the new drive-in theatres for a science fiction or horror double feature.

As with every major American city, San Jose's entertainment needs were eagerly met by entrepreneurs who saw economic opportunity in affordable entertainment. Most of these exhibitors would not become famous outside their own locale, but a select few would move on to find considerable fame and fortune elsewhere, ultimately attaining national recognition via Hollywood.

In the early years of the 20th century, once San Jose's entertainment began to outgrow the converted meeting halls and storefronts that were its first theatres, the showmen turned to skilled architects, some of them local and some of wider renown, to design venues that would lift the image of San Jose's entertainment to a more respectable and refined level. This ushered in the era of the movie palace, and while San Jose's finest theatres were not the 3,000-, 4,000-, or even 5,000-seat temples of art and showmanship found in San Francisco, Los Angeles, the Midwest, or the East Coast, the best of them were likely the most impressive and luxurious buildings available to the population of this agricultural capital at the time.

As suburbia became an American phenomenon, downtowns all across the nation began to decline, and San Jose's was no exception. The decision by Macy's to locate at Valley Fair—San Jose's first major shopping development—signaled a vast change in the city's image. San Jose grew to become a decentralized city. Soon entertainment followed, with new theatres and drive-ins springing up along the major commercial thoroughfares, which had only decades before been dirt roads connecting San Jose with the smaller rural communities of the valley.

With the transition of San Jose from an agricultural to a technological hub, its economic focus was scattered across the Santa Clara Valley, ultimately to be more commonly known as Silicon Valley. Downtown, with its legacy of older buildings, was struggling to reinvent itself. As the 1960s and 1970s unfolded, large swaths of San Jose's heart were leveled, taking many theatres in the process. The era of the suburban multiplex had arrived, and by this time, the theatres of downtown were hardly relevant. Those in San Jose's neighborhoods and in surrounding smaller city centers fared little better, either being converted to other commercial uses or demolished. Occasionally one would carry on for a time, showing classic, foreign, or independent films or locally produced live entertainment, and a couple of them survive on such a policy today.

Happily, San Jose has benefited in the last two decades by an increased awareness of and respect for all aspects of its history, and its remaining theatres from the first half of the 20th century, though a precious few, have lasted long enough to be widely appreciated. Just as vital are the efforts to make these architectural treasures hold their own in a contemporary culture where art and taste have become ever more varied and transitory. Nevertheless, whether it is an old stage theatre built when electricity was new, and now showcasing cutting-edge comedy, or a movie palace resounding with operatic triumph, or the revival of a wide-screen epic in one of suburbia's first domed cinemas, it is yet possible to find audiences who come together to experience a special event in a special place. San Jose still preserves a fine legacy of theatre buildings, both in those that stand and in those that survive only in photographs and memories.

The modern theatrical venues established since the 1960s, along with a thriving local theatrical and musical scene that reflects an ever more varied San Jose culture, are making their own history, which will no doubt one day be chronicled in words and images. These theatres are beyond the scope of this volume, as are the dozens of multi-screened cinemas that now blanket the Silicon Valley of today. You are now invited to savor the San Jose theatres of another time. Enjoy the view from your seat!

One

EARLY STAGES AND
5¢ SCREENS

From the time San Jose was officially established on November 29, 1777, until the 1850s, there appears to be no evidence of stage entertainment being part of the early life of the city. James and Sarah Kirby Stark opened the Stark Theatre at 46 North First Street in 1859, successfully presenting Shakespeare and other refined offerings designed to give San Jose's often rough-and-tumble citizenry diversions of a healthy sort. Despite the Stark's closure by 1867, a trend had begun. New theatres began opening in rapid succession. The Music Hall, at 48 North First Street, and the Opera House, on Santa Clara Street between Second and Third Streets, both opened in 1870. The latter could boast of a 10-piece orchestra and the presentation of traveling operatic and dramatic troupes. There were at least four others, including the California and Garden Theatres, whose names would echo in completely new structures built elsewhere in town decades later.

Movie theatres arrived with the conversion of the former Methodist church at 23 North Second Street to the Empire Theatre in about 1900. Most of San Jose's earliest theatres presented movies on the same program as vaudeville acts. Live comedians, singers, acrobats, magicians, and dancers might find themselves on the same bill as short comedic, romantic, or dramatic film offerings accompanied by a pianist or a handful of musicians. During this time, the nickelodeon craze was sweeping an America that could not seem to get its fill of pictures that moved. The usual admission price, a nickel, was combined with a Greek word for performance hall to create the term "nickelodeon," but in many cases, the definition of a performance hall or theatre was stretched quite thinly. These movie theatres were typically converted storefronts.

Today not a trace of these earliest theatres remains. While many of them were still running, two new theatres opened that foreshadowed the years to come, the Victory and the Jose. The first would last over 60 years and go out with blazing suddenness. The second would last long enough to become new again.

James D. Phelan, real estate developer and politician, hired San Francisco architects Curlett and McCaw in 1897 to design the San Jose Theatre. Plans were filed with the city in March 1898. By the time of its opening in 1899 with the play *The School for Scandal*, the name had been changed to the Victory Theatre in honor of Adm. George Dewey's Manila Bay victory in the Spanish-American War. (Steve Levin.)

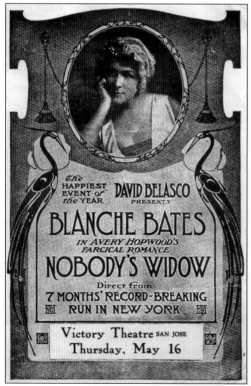

Notable players to tread the Victory's stage included Sarah Bernhardt, Ethel Barrymore, and George M. Cohan. Famed female impersonator Julian Eltinge appeared in *Fascinating Widow*. This art nouveau–style handbill advertises the actress Blanche Bates. *Nobody's Widow* fascinated audiences in New York and doubtlessly did the same in San Jose. (History San Jose.)

This early photograph shows the ample size of the Victory's stage. In front is an orchestra pit large enough for perhaps a dozen musicians. Onstage, a series of painted scenic drops create a classical garden party scene for the formally attired couples dancing or seated at tables. The fellow seated in the center is dressed a bit incongruously as either a pharaoh or a genie. (History San Jose.)

The earthquake that shook San Francisco on April 18, 1906, did the same to San Jose. In this postcard view, the Victory's ticket lobby, which was open to the street, shows its share of damage. The lobby skylight and the wood and stained-glass paneled box office visible behind the fallen planks required major repairs. Note the potted palm trees, a popular theatre lobby embellishment. (Steve Levin.)

In 1918, all San Jose theatres were closed as a result of the Spanish flu epidemic. Before long though, audiences were able to flock in once again. In this 1920s view, children pack the house. By this time, movies were part of the show at the Victory. (John C. Gordon Collection; Special Collections and Archives, San Jose State University.)

In 1935, the Victory was given a completely new exterior design in what we now call the art deco style. Theodore M. "Ted" Newman, formerly a business manager for Golden State Theatre Corporation, later entered the insurance business, photographing theatres for appraisal purposes all over California and western Nevada between 1942 and 1945. Here is a tour of the Victory through his camera lens. (Steve Levin.)

By the time Ted Newman took this photograph in 1944, the outer lobby skylight was long gone. A new wall had been built to frame the entrance doors, and popcorn, then a new addition to the movie-going experience, was here to stay. (Steve Levin.)

A 180-degree turn by the photographer shows the long, narrow slope of the lobby. In 1944, the heirs of original builder James Phelan sold the Victory to San Jose Amusement Company, headed by James B. Lima, Walter J. Preddy, and Ben Levin. Although movies were the chief attraction, the stage was still used, as evidenced by the poster advertising "Eddie's Amateur Contest Every Friday Nite." (Steve Levin.)

This photograph shows that the Victory lobby was still a place of comfort. It needed to be, as it was a 97-foot march from the sidewalk to the auditorium! Overstuffed sofas and gracious floor lamps provided a touch of home, while the lively floral-patterned carpet added both elegance and practicality, as popcorn and soda spills were less noticeable on a carpet pattern such as this. (Steve Levin.)

In Ted Newman's view of the stage, the original 1899 curtains, together with any trace of the garden scene, have been relegated to history. Instead, layers of simple, plush fabric hang in their place. The movie screen is likely behind the rearmost curtain. Original plaster ornament still frames the stage, and a clock is mounted at the base. (Steve Levin.)

Here, in this and the following photograph, is the view of the Victory's auditorium from the stage. Its seating capacity in 1935 is listed as 1,500 spread between the main floor and two balconies. The upper balcony originally contained simple wood benches. Above the balcony was a dome ringed by bare lightbulbs. In 1899, these lights celebrated the novelty of electricity. (Steve Levin.)

This photograph clearly shows the cast-iron pillars that supported both balconies. The original 1899 plaster shields and garlands fronting the balconies were painted in a monochrome coat over the original metal-leaf finishes. All across the rear of the main floor can be seen curtains, which could be drawn aside for standees in the event of a full house. (Steve Levin.)

15

MAIN ELEVATION   SIDE VIEW

VICTORY THEATRE
SAN JOSE   CALIFORNIA
SAN JOSE AMUSEMENT CO   O.A. DEICHMANN-ARCHITECT
· OWNERS ·   1016 Market st. S.F. 2. Calif
25. Taylor st. San Francisco Calif.   · Feb. 15. 46 ·

Between the lucrative movie business of the war years and the decrease in attendance because of television in the early 1950s, many ideas surfaced for building new theatres and remodeling existing ones. One such project was a plan for a new Victory Theatre to replace the old. San Francisco architect Otto A. Deichmann's office produced the following two renderings of the new theatre. Note the size of the penciled man for scale. (Steve Levin.)

While Deichmann's design for the facade would have resulted in one of the Bay Area's most distinctive theatre exteriors of the 1940s, the interior would have been more typical of the period. This project was not to be. Instead, not long after a "Gay 90s" 50th anniversary stage show, the theatre simply received a new marquee and name, Crest, and became strictly a movie theatre. (Steve Levin.)

16

The Victory would live as the Crest for another decade and a half. On June 6, 1965, it all ended dramatically. According to the *San Jose Mercury*, a police officer on Market Street spotted smoke curling from under the roof at 8:57 a.m. Soon fire district Chief Robert True had men and equipment heading to the theatre. Here flames and smoke burst above the north sidewall of the auditorium. (Steve Levin.)

Chief True called a second alarm. A third followed at 9:33 a.m. with a fourth about 40 minutes later. In this view, thick smoke rises above the stage house. The parking lot in the foreground, which served the theatre, retained the Crest's earlier name. A sign identifies the lot as Victory Parking today, although the 25¢ hourly rate has passed, like the theatre itself, into history. (Steve Levin.)

17

Citizens crowded the sidewalks. Patrons at the adjacent Angelus Hotel were roused from bed by firemen. A squad broke their way into the lobby, but as soon as they reached the auditorium, they were confronted by an inferno and had to back away. It was decided to confine the fire to the building. Soon the roof collapsed onto the balconies and flames climbed over 100 feet into the air. (Steve Levin.)

The flames consume the wood structure of the stage fly tower in this view. For several hours, combined hoses, pouring 2,000 gallons of water a minute, were directed at the fire. (Steve Levin.)

After the flames died down, firemen continued to douse hot spots. Here remnants of the auditorium sidewalls cling to the brick shell, exposed to view on what was otherwise a clear day. In the distance, the domes of St. Joseph's Church (now St. Joseph's Cathedral) glint in the sun. (Steve Levin.)

Water is aimed at a hot spot in this photograph of the back of the auditorium. The shaft-like structure against this wall was hollow and never used. It has been speculated that it may have been intended to house an elevator. In the distance on the right stands the Hotel De Anza with its original neon rooftop sign, still a beacon today at Market and Santa Clara Streets. (Steve Levin.)

Fire hoses snake into the long lobby as the mop-up continues. Had movie-going not taken such a hit from television, and had downtown San Jose not faced heavy competition from the commerce of the suburbs, perhaps this marquee would have once again lit up, beckoning patrons back to a rebuilt Crest. It was not to be. The building was insured, however, and damage was set at $400,000. (Steve Levin.)

Gary Markley, the Crest's janitor, had left the theatre at 5:30 a.m. and noticed no sign of trouble. There were many theatre fires started by cigarette butts falling through vents and then smoldering inside the wooden balcony structure for a time before fully igniting. Such could have been the cause of the Crest fire. This view looks toward where the balconies stood. (Steve Levin.)

A complete document detailing the replacement cost to rebuild the theatre to identical pre-fire condition was drawn up. It was never acted upon. Looking down into the auditorium, the proscenium arch frames fallen bricks and ashes where once four real horses galloped on a treadmill for the chariot race scene in a live production of *Ben Hur* and where, many decades later, the Beatles would appear on-screen. (Steve Levin.)

Looking through a side doorway, a completely intact iron balcony support column remains. Behind it, the decorative iron aisle standards of seat rows carry a new burden—heaps of debris. (Steve Levin.)

Wrecking cranes were soon brought to the site to knock down the stage house walls, which were in danger of collapsing. Compare this view with that on page 17, bottom. The two structures to the right of the theatre ruins, the arch-windowed Knights of Columbus Building and the taller Commercial Building, still stand today. (Steve Levin.)

The marquee is blank, the poster cases empty. No more Cash Nite, no more Ten-O-Win games. The vertical sign would be carefully taken down and re-lettered to find a new life as the main sign for the Jose Theatre, which it remains today. The rest of James Phelan's old Victory Theatre would be reduced to rubble. (Steve Levin.)

On February 7, 1903, the Unique Theatre opened at 20–26 East Santa Clara Street, adjacent to where the former Bank of Italy/Bank of America tower stands. Sidney Patrick "Sid" Grauman was proprietor, and the theatre was part of the Sullivan-Considine vaudeville circuit. The Unique opened with a French poodle act, dancing and singing acts, an African American quartet, and a comedy sketch, followed by movies, all for 10¢. (History San Jose.)

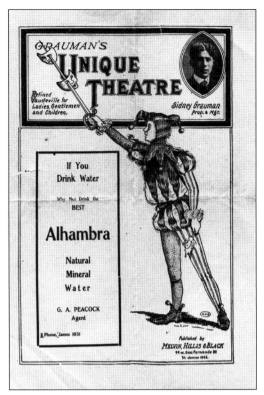

French poodles notwithstanding, the Unique's brief career gave rise to superstars. Roscoe "Fatty" Arbuckle, who was the theatre's ticket taker and mop boy, starting at $35 a week plus one free dinner, went on to fame in silent movies. Al Jolson, who debuted onstage at $75 a week, truly reached renown in vaudeville and recording and reached his career pinnacle as the most famous first voice of sound movies. (History San Jose.)

The Grauman name had been removed from the signage by the time the 1906 earthquake removed nearly everything but the sign. The projection booth stands exposed in this photograph by Hank Calloway. Sid Grauman soon opened Grauman's Imperial Theatre, an adult entertainment venue in San Francisco, which still stands as the Market Street Cinema. Sid would head to Los Angeles, finding success with his Million Dollar, Egyptian, and Chinese Theatres. (History San Jose.)

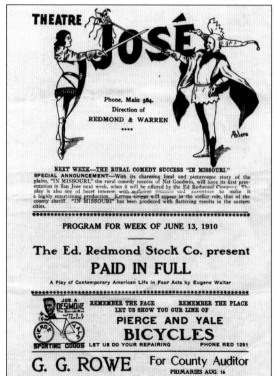

The Victory/Crest burned and the Unique tumbled down, but the Jose is still with us. Entrepreneur David Jacks is best known as the name behind Monterey Jack cheese. Among his real estate ventures was this theatre, opened in 1904. Eugene Walters's *Paid in Full* is advertised as "a play of Contemporary American Life in Four Acts." The coming attraction, *In Missouri*, enjoyed "flattering results" in the eastern United States. (History San Jose.)

The Jose, with a facade of tan brick, Mediterranean palazzo-style ornamentation, and art nouveau wrought-iron railings, was designed by architect William Binder. He would later partner with Ernest N. Curtis to design several other theatres for San Jose. In this photograph of the new theatre, citizens pose in their best attire along with two well-behaved canines. The sign was moved over the sidewalk when the theatre was open. (History San Jose.)

By today's standards, the Jose had a small stage, but at the time, it served perfectly well for a theatre of around 800 seats. Here the Jose's orchestra poses on the stage. Leo Sullivan, violinist and orchestra leader, is seated at the far left. His handwritten memoirs of more than 20 years onstage in San Jose preserve stories that otherwise may have been lost. (History San Jose.)

Leo Sullivan recounted the appearance at the Jose of two elephants housed in a nearby warehouse, which was being used to store bags of cement. The elephants began spraying each other playfully with cement. There was no time to clean off their white "coats," so the curtain went up and the dusty elephants appeared as the orchestra played *March of the Mighty Pachyderms*. Here an all-human cast poses. (History San Jose.)

Plays gave way to vaudeville and then movies. In this 1935 view, a lightbulb and neon vertical sign and a sporty art deco marquee have replaced the original swing-out sign and red tile canopy. The building to the left of the theatre became the home of Allen's Furniture and today houses Zanotto's Market. (John C. Gordon Collection; Special Collections and Archives, San Jose State University.)

Insurance photographer Ted Newman made two visits to the Jose. This first view is from 1942. He would return in 1944 to more thoroughly document the theatre. A group of six boys and two girls stand outside. Judging by the boys' stance—hands on hips, legs sturdily apart—they have just seen Charles Starret and Russell Hayden in *West of Tombstone*. (Steve Levin.)

Here begins Ted Newman's 1944 photographic account of the Jose. The war was on and movie attendance was high, even for a revival of the 1937 Tex Ritter hit *Trouble in Texas*, in which the cowboy singer unravels the mystery of how and why rodeo stars are being killed with poisoned needles. Lighter fun was had in the 1943 Freddy Martin/Ann Miller musical *What's Buzzin', Cousin?* (Steve Levin.)

By this time, the Jose's lobby had been modernized. The ornamental moldings above are survivors from 1904, but the staircase railings speak moderne. Aside from the carpet and the addition of a new doorway in the far wall, this view remains the same today, minus, of course, the war bonds poster. (Steve Levin.)

Turning right around, four pairs of entrance doors set into a curved wall lead to the exterior ticket lobby. The wrought-iron chandelier and the moderne trough light may not blend with each other, but they represent the "latest thing" of their respective eras and still provide their ambient light today. (Steve Levin.)

This is a view of the auditorium from the balcony. The ornamental proscenium arch is the product of a remodel, probably in the 1920s. The original had been curved and flanked by box seats. Not long after this photograph was taken, the proscenium was redone yet again to the squared-off design it has today. (Steve Levin.)

As viewed from the stage, the Jose's auditorium had changed very little through the years and appears much the same today, although original sculpted torches and garlands from 1904 have been replicated on the face of the balcony rail. Note the smudges on the downstairs back wall over each seat, the consequence of men's hair products of the day. (Steve Levin.)

In this photograph, the balcony shows evidence of heavy use. Wear on the upholstery and a scuffed balcony rail attest to the life of a then 40-year-old theatre. There were more years of heavy use ahead for the venerable showplace. (Steve Levin.)

In this *c.* 1962 photograph, a revival of the 1956 *Autumn Leaves* is paired with Marlon Brando and Trevor Howard in their respective Fletcher Christian and Captain Bligh roles in *Mutiny on the Bounty*. Despite the prevalence of concession counters in theatres, milk shakes and hamburgers were available at the fountain to the left, still serving them up after over 25 years. (History San Jose.)

Still packing them in when this 1982 photograph was taken, the Jose had established itself as the home of triple features at bargain prices. Paul Newman in *Fort Apache, The Bronx* balances out the bill, while the two other titles assault the screen with drug lords, female and female-impersonating kung fu masters, and an obese psychic to boot. The marquee and sign are nicely painted, and the neon is in complete working order. More years would pass and the Jose would finally be closed, General Theatrical Company having sold the house in 1988. As a survivor of both the 1906 and 1989 earthquakes, there was fear that the Jose might not stand another, and the lights went out in 1991. (Gary Lee Parks.)

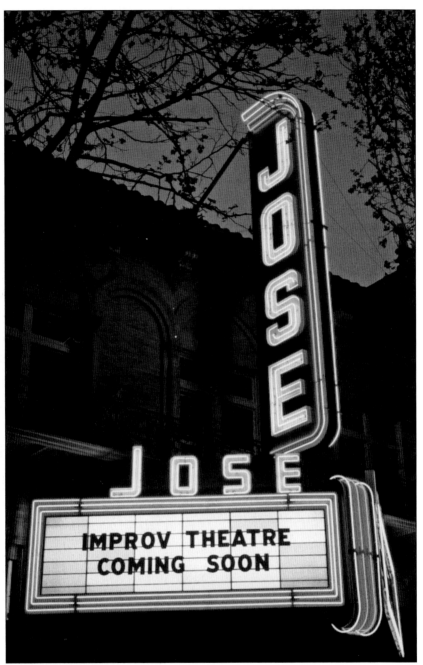

It was not to be the end for the Jose. The 1990s saw the Preservation Action Council of San Jose, as well as other groups and individuals, fight to see the theatre seismically retrofitted, refurbished, and put to a new use. The neon marquee was also fought for, and the vertical sign, having once been part of the long-gone Crest (ex-Victory) Theatre, was also seen as significant. By 2002, the Jose's new life began as the South Bay outpost of the improv comedy circuit. Today patrons drink and dine in a terraced auditorium while top-name comedians entertain on the stage where Al Jolson and Harry Houdini once appeared, amid the ambience that can be found only in San Jose's oldest operating theatre. (Martin Schmidt.)

In 1910, the Lyric Theatre opened at 61 South Second Street, across from the Jose. A nickelodeon beginning as did others of its kind, showing a program of short subjects that changed several times a week, it outlived downtown's other nickel showplaces by a substantial margin. The Lieber Sign painting studio operated not only its business upstairs, but the theatre itself. (History San Jose.)

Both of these early views of the Lyric date from 1914. In this photograph, the Lieber Sign studio windows are visible. A banner over the box office and entry doors proclaims the Lyric as an outlet for Mutual Movies, which "make time fly." *A Barrier Royal* with Walter Belasco and *The Warning Cry*, a short with Francelia Billington, were both released in 1914. Note the sculpted lion head at the center of the arch. (Jack Tillmany.)

With his camera, Ted Newman preserved a rarity. The Lyric was a nickelodeon, still going strong (though not for a nickel per ticket) by the 1940s. The only exterior change of note is a swing-out sign of neon to replace the original all-lightbulb unit. Lieber Signs is still upstairs. *In Old California* is playing. The Lyric would operate until 1960. Today the site is a parking lot. (Steve Levin.)

The Market Street, which opened in 1912 across from St. Joseph's Church, was the direct opposite of the Lyric where longevity was concerned. It appears again in the 1913 city directory but then vanishes. The Liberty Theatre would open immediately to the south. In this photograph, the transition of San Jose's streets from equestrian to automobile traffic is evident. (Jack Tillmany.)

Two

SAN JOSE'S FINEST ENTERTAINMENT

As the 20th century got well underway, movies became big business. The live vaudeville acts that so often were part of the show began to lose prominence or to evolve into traveling "unit" (or packaged) stage revues exclusive to specific theatre chains. Yes, movies and vaudeville had gone corporate, and movie theatres themselves followed suit, through there were plenty of local and regional theatre companies jockeying for the pick of the product. The main regional chains to secure San Jose strongholds at first were Ackerman and Harris and Turner and Dahnken (T&D). Ackerman and Harris built theatres on the peninsula and in San Francisco. The T&D chain ultimately encompassed dozens of theatres in Central and Northern California. San Jose gained its first deluxe theatre devoted chiefly to movies, appropriately named Theatre DeLuxe, courtesy of Turner and Dahnken. The T&D circuit became such an attractive plum that it was purchased in 1924 by Sol Lesser of West Coast Theatres. West Coast was a chain of theatres incorporated in 1920 by combining the interests of the Gore Brothers, Adolph Ramish, and Sol Lesser.

Local showman James Beatty would control additional premiere showplaces, building the Liberty and taking over David Jacks's Jose and Ackerman and Harris's Hippodrome. Beatty also founded the National Theatre Syndicate, which included 19 theatres in Northern California.

There was no shortage of architectural skill to fulfill the dreams of the theatre business. Unlike many architects employed by theatre chains nationally who designed structures regionally or nationwide, those who designed theatres built in San Jose during the golden years of downtown showmanship were local, that is, based in the Bay Area. San Jose's own William Binder and partner Ernest N. Curtis got the lion's share of the commissions. Charles Peter Weeks and William Day, working from San Francisco, codesigned the Hippodrome with Binder and Curtis, and then worked their own magic with the "new" California (see chapter three). Alexander Cantin and son McKenzie would add their tribute to the postwar moderne style in the Studio, the last of the big downtown movie houses.

When T&D's Theatre DeLuxe opened in 1912, a contest was held to determine how to pronounce the name. Would it be "DeLucks" or "DeLukes"? "DeLukes" won. The more common "DeLucks" is the one that stuck with everyday folks. This 1917 postcard view shows a South First Street that has largely vanished. The five-story Twohy Building on the right and the six-balconied Hotel Montgomery on the left remain. (History San Jose.)

As day turns into evening, the lights blink on as the DeLuxe presents an early retelling of the Davy Crockett legend, plus another offering, *Rose of the World*. The man on the far right with the megaphone has dressed appropriately for the Crockett movie. Likely he is part of a publicity stunt. (John C. Gordon Collection; Special Collections and Archives, San Jose State University.)

In this photograph from the theatre's early years, a throng of moviegoers is captured for posterity. In 1913, adult admission was 10¢ and children got in for 5¢. The 500-seat balcony was 5¢ for all ages. The program changed four times a week. The air changed every three minutes, thanks to a state-of-the-art circulation system. The 32-musician orchestra was a big hit. (John C. Gordon Collection; Special Collections and Archives, San Jose State University.)

By the time 1921's *Hail the Woman*, with Florence Vidor, graced the screen, the name DeLuxe had given way to simply T&D. Binder and Curtis designed this theatre. Note the prominent fire escapes. Safety in theatre design had become a foremost concern. (John C. Gordon Collection; Special Collections and Archives, San Jose State University.)

In 1924, like several T&D houses acquired by West Coast Theatres, this one was renamed the California. A series of identical vertical signs, outlined and topped by California poppies wrought in twinkling lightbulbs, was created for these theatres. On the far left is the vertical sign of Beatty's American Theatre, and in the distance, the Bank of Italy tower takes shape. (Steve Levin.)

The year 1927 brought the theatre's fourth and final name, the Mission. "Tired Tim," theatre cat, took up residence at the Mission. He would wander slowly across the stage about half an hour before the last picture was over and lie down on top of the organ console. When the theatre closed for the night, Tim would be given milk, and then he spent the night chasing mice. (Jack Tillmany.)

On March 18, 1928, the Mission held the Santa Clara Valley premiere of *The Jazz Singer* and movies with sound were here to stay. A decade later, *Gone With the Wind* played a record four-week run. Despite successes such as these, plus an art deco remodeling, the Mission closed in July 1952. In this 1942 Ted Newman photograph, the sandwich shop still bears the theatre's original name, DeLuxe. (Steve Levin.)

As this 1916 photograph attests, large theatres designed mainly for movies were a recipe for success. Binder and Curtis, after designing the DeLuxe for T&D, were hired by showman James Beatty to design the Liberty, which opened in 1914 at 67 Market Street. Jan Schinahan accompanied the movies on the Morton theatre pipe organ. (John C. Gordon Collection; Special Collections and Archives, San Jose State University.)

In this view from the balcony, the details of the auditorium are displayed. A ceiling of pressed tin houses ventilator grilles from which hang chandeliers shaded in fabric. The walls are painted to resemble blocks of stone and are accented with stenciling in imitation of tapestries. The grilles fronting the organ pipes house statuary, and the three-manual organ console commands a view of the screen. (John C. Gordon Collection; Special Collections and Archives, San Jose State University.)

Here is the Morton organ console, plus organist. He is playing *The Wedding of the Painted Doll*, featured in *Broadway Melody of 1929*. After talking pictures arrived, the organ was no longer needed, and owner James Beatty facilitated its removal to Grace Baptist Church, where it is the only original San Jose theatre organ to remain in its home city. (John C. Gordon Collection; Special Collections and Archives, San Jose State University.)

Photographer Ted Newman was on the scene in 1942 and again in 1944. Through his lens, it is possible to tour the Liberty. The "two first run hits" are *Bowery at Midnight*, with Bela Lugosi, and *The Living Ghost*, concerning a zombie with half a brain. The golden age of horror was underway and the Liberty was not going to miss out. (Steve Levin.)

In addition to monsters and ghosts, it was natural for the war years to bring titles like *Pacific Hitler* and *Submarine Base* to the Liberty. They add a jarring note among the original 1914 lobby ornamentation. Carved wooden tables and chairs retain elegance, while Old Glory helps instill patriotism. (Steve Levin.)

Turning around, it is easy to see the steep incline that led to the inner lobby. From the sidewalk to the front doors, one walked upon a floor of white and blue honeycomb-patterned tiles. Carpet continued up the slope and throughout the theatre. A drinking fountain is sandwiched between the two inner entry doorways, and to the left, a cigarette vending machine tempts patrons with the promise of added relaxation. (Steve Levin.)

In 1944, the Liberty's auditorium looks much the same as it did in 1914. All decorations have been repainted though, and chandeliers of likely 1920s vintage have replaced the originals. The orchestra pit has been filled in for the addition of a few more seats. The decoration in this photograph would ultimately be ripped out to make way for a larger screen. (Steve Levin.)

This view shows the theatre wearing her age well. A few seat backs have been reupholstered in non-matching material, and smudges line the back wall where men have leaned their heads. Space was at a premium in a theatre as long and narrow as the Liberty, so the rear of the balcony is asymmetrical, and even the projection booth is off-center. (Steve Levin.)

In 1976, under the tenure of Spanish-language movie exhibitor Jose Borges, the Liberty was renamed the Mexico. After closure, the Mexico signs were transferred to the former Esquire Theatre on Santa Clara Street. The Liberty name was revealed once more. Wreckers descended in October 1982. Bricks were cleaned and salvaged by the palette load, and much of the auditorium ceiling found new life at Teske's Germania restaurant. (Jack Tillmany.)

The Hippodrome was built at 261 South First Street. A part of the Ackerman and Harris circuit, the house of over 1,600 seats was the largest yet in San Jose. It was operated in association with Loew's Theatres, a major player on the East Coast but not nearly as influential in the West. D. Ben Levin was the manager, and Harold Rea held forth at the organ. (John C. Gordon; Special Collections and Archives, San Jose State University.)

In this early photograph, an organist is at the console of the two-manual, four-rank Wurlitzer player organ, which could be played live or with player piano-style rolls. Wurlitzer made well over 500 such instruments, but fewer than 10 survive intact and of those only two or three are in use. (John C. Gordon Collection; Special Collections and Archives, San Jose State University.)

Local showman James Beatty took over operation in 1922, and Loew's Hippodrome became Beatty's American. Sculpted detailing surrounds an immense window illuminating a lofty ticket lobby. Urns and finials top delicate Gothic spindle-like engaged columns. The facade was tinted in at least three colors. If this looks familiar today, it should be noted that Binder and Curtis designed this theatre in association with Weeks and Day, who would later design the "new" California, a block to the south, along similar lines. (John C. Gordon Collection; Special Collections and Archives, San Jose State University.)

Herman Kersken, the American Theatre's manager under James Beatty, may or may not have arranged the location shoot shown underway in this photograph, but it is the type of publicity stunt that could ensure a theatre manager a long and prosperous career. Kersken would have just such a career in San Jose. (John C. Gordon Collection; Special Collections and Archives, San Jose State University.)

In sharp contrast to the earlier photograph of young boys in front of the theatre, a more mature audience waits in an orderly line. Three heavy milk-glass pendant light fixtures hang from the marquee soffit. Down the sidewalk, a sign reading "DeLuxe Rooms" advertises a rooming house named for the Theatre DeLuxe across the street. (John C. Gordon Collection; Special Collections and Archives, San Jose State University.)

A new streamlined neon vertical sign and marquee invite patrons to play Bingo and see *Nothing but the Truth* and *Appointment for Love* at the State Theatre. But this is the former American, merely given an up-to-date 1938 remodeling. Once again, it is possible to join Ted Newman for a 1942 look-see. (Steve Levin.)

Towering facades usually lead to lofty lobbies. Here the original vaulted ceiling of 1919 remains, but the sculpted capitals on the pilasters are new. Stenciled patterns in the style that would eventually be named art deco provide a perfect match for hanging fixtures and wall sconces of wrought sheet metal and etched glass. (Steve Levin.)

Here is the lobby as seen looking back toward the entrance. Velvet ropes await the crowds, which will gather to await the usher's announcement of available seats. The reader board seems to be in the process of being changed. Above the letters, a mural depicts a barely clad goddess in a four-horse chariot, cape billowing behind her. (Steve Levin.)

The inner lobby of a theatre usually nestles under the rear portion of the balcony structure. As a result, a more intimate space is created. The mezzanine level was a perfect place for patrons who might feel the need to leave the auditorium for a few quiet moments. Here an overstuffed couch, a vending machine, and cigarette urns invite patrons to linger. (Steve Levin.)

A grand piano, surrounded by a comfortable sofa and chairs, creates an intimate salon-like haven from the crowds that so often milled about the lobby. Note that the carpet pattern is different upstairs than in the main lobby. Oftentimes a theatre would be re-carpeted only where and when needed, occasionally resulting in an eclectic mix of carpet patterns as the years wore on. (Steve Levin.)

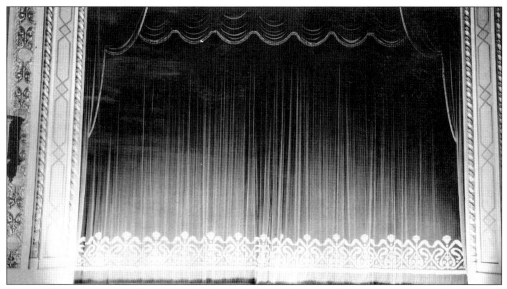

One wishes perhaps that Newman had included a wider view of the auditorium in his lens, but at least he detailed the curtain clearly. Neither it nor the elegant proscenium frame seems to have received the art deco treatment given to the rest of the theatre, likely a matter of budget. (Steve Levin.)

By literally taping together two photographs, Ted Newman was able to give a sense of the tremendous size and height of the State's auditorium. This was certainly appropriate for a theatre once called the Hippodrome, a name dating back to antiquity that was typically reserved for theatres and arenas of far greater size. In addition to the colorful art deco patterns applied to the original ceiling and Gothic vaults, acoustical tiles can be seen covering the front of the balcony and the wall above the balcony rear, a necessary addition when movies began to talk. (Steve Levin.)

The theatre received one final name change. The existing vertical sign and marquee were re-lettered with the UA logo of United Artists Theatres. The facade was painted bright red, and the signage was white with red letters. Twin sculpted masks still grimaced on both top corners, lonely remnants of the opulent Hippodrome. The movie titles shown here, like the theatre, have gone completely modern. (Steve Levin.)

In this 1950s photograph, the tall stage house of the old Hippodrome soars skyward. The letters "UA" are spaced where the name "State" once was. The Redevelopment Agency of San Jose bought the theatre, and there was discussion of reusing it as a community performance facility, but in 1976 it closed, fixtures and equipment were auctioned, and demolition ensued for a parking lot, which is still there. (History San Jose.)

Fox West Coast opened the Padre a few doors north of the American Theatre in 1933. It was a simple theatre hollowed out of a 19th-century commercial building that had once housed the Adler 15¢ Store. In this 1942 photograph, the Padre's marquee and vertical sign display one of San Jose's finest examples of the neon sign glass bender's art. (Jack Tillmany.)

When this 1945 photograph was taken, management was doing its part for the war effort, advertising war bonds as many theatres did. Over the box office, *Steppin' in Society*, with Edward Everett Horton, and two-time Oscar winner *National Velvet*, with Mickey Rooney and Elizabeth Taylor, are prominently advertised to passersby. (Jack Tillmany.)

Patrons line up to see Randolph Scott in *Return of the Bad Men*, a Western in which frontier Oklahoma is plagued by 10 killers, led by a lady called Cheyenne. With it is *French Leave*, a romantic comedy set in the port of Marseilles. This 1948 photograph shows the marquee sporting a new milk-glass reader board in place of the old metal and glass moveable letters. (Jack Tillmany.)

In 1957, Cecil B. DeMille's *The Ten Commandments* enjoyed an 18-week run at the Padre. In the early 1960s, Fox West Coast Theatres considered a complete overhaul of the theatre, which would have renamed it the Capri, a name as popular in the 1960s as Crest was in the 1940s. Instead, on June 1, 1965, the Padre closed. The Fairmont Hotel stands on the site today. (History San Jose.)

The carved inscription over the entrance may read "Municipal Auditorium," but this multipurpose structure at San Carlos and Market Streets has long been called Civic Auditorium. Developed by T. S. Montgomery and built in 1934, the Civic and the adjacent Montgomery Theater (visible at the far end of this 1934 photograph) are the best known works of architects Binder and Curtis designed for public assembly. (History San Jose.)

The Civic Auditorium appears today almost exactly as it did when it opened. Never restored, it has simply been used and maintained. The cavernous hall, with its stadium seats, hardwood floor, proscenium stage, and art deco organ grilles (fronting pipe chambers never filled), has hosted concerts, rallies, and political events and was a prime convention location until the opening of the McEnery Convention Center across the street in the 1980s. (Gary Lee Parks.)

Architects referenced sourcebooks of historical patterns for their ornamentation. Perhaps this explains the resemblance of the Civic's arched entrance to the longer beachfront arcade of architect William H. Weeks's 1907 Casino at Santa Cruz's Boardwalk, down to the squat Corinthian columns with their smiling faces. Whether Binder and Curtis were aware of this is unknown, and the stucco faces have been missing from the Santa Cruz Casino since the 1950s. (Gary Lee Parks.)

The Montgomery Theater is entered through a little courtyard along Market Street. Named after its developer, the Montgomery has been a home for all kinds of community events that have needed an intimate theatrical setting. The Gilbert and Sullivan Society of San Jose (now the Lyric Theatre) has called the venue its home for decades. Opera San Jose did likewise until its 2004 move to the restored California Theatre. (Gary Lee Parks.)

While a Spanish Colonial theme dominates the Civic Auditorium and Montgomery Theater, accents in the art deco mode do appear. In this 1934 photograph, these are visible in the carpet pattern and the ventilation grilles. Today the decorative urns are gone and the walls are painted a darker color, but the original chandeliers still hang, and busts of indigenous Californians and helmeted Conquistadores look down from the walls. (History San Jose.)

The Gay Theatre opened in 1949 on the southwest corner of First and San Salvador Streets in a 1913 building that had formerly housed the Boschken Motor Company. Murals on the auditorium walls featured Parisian street scenes. Here, in 1955, young moviegoers crowd the ticket lobby for an exclusive showing of the musical *Guys and Dolls* with Marlon Brando, Jean Simmons, and Frank Sinatra. (Steve Levin.)

In the 1960s, exhibitor Mason Shaw ran a policy of foreign films, but by the 1970s, under new ownership, the theatre was screening "guys" and "dolls" in far more specialized situations. In this 1979 photograph, patrons are invited to see adult movie superstar Vanessa Del Rio in *New York Babes* and John Leslie and Juliet Anderson in *Shoppe of Temptations*. (Jack Tillmany.)

The year 1989 saw the conversion of the Gay Theatre into the first of a long and sometimes rapid succession of nightclub incarnations, the F/X Club. The marquee was given new neon colors and made to animate festively. In this 2008 photograph, the former theatre still wears its most recent sequined "party dress" as Angels Ultra Lounge but is now closed and vacant. (Gary Lee Parks.)

In 1930, plans were announced for a $225,000, 1,500-seat theatre to be built by United Artists on the northeast corner of First and San Salvador Streets. Its moderne facade would have featured the trademark "Unity" and "Artistry" allegorical figures. It was not built. In 1950, the Studio, built and operated by Richard Borg, made its debut. This view dates from 1957. (Jack Tillmany.)

The 900-seat Studio, designed by Alexander Cantin, likely with assistance from his son McKenzie, opened with the movie *Fancy Pants*. In this 1965 photograph, *The Liquidator*, a spoof on the spy movies so popular at the time, is paired with *The Yellow Rolls Royce*, a romantic comedy set in Europe. (Steve Levin.)

As downtown slid into decline, the Studio tried, in 1973 and 1974, a policy of adult films to compete with the Pussycat Theatre across San Salvador Street. Next a policy of second-run triple features followed before a diet of films from Spanish-speaking countries around the world carried the day. In the early 1990s, the policy changed to second-run Hollywood product in a double-feature format. In this 1990 view, the neon glows as brightly as in 1950. The letters are white and burn steadily. The crest at the top, along with the horizontal bands between the letters, is magenta. These have animated in several ways over the years. (Gary Lee Parks.)

At the end of the decade, following a special screening as part of San Jose's Cinequest film festival, the Studio closed to become yet another nightclub. The auditorium's murals of ballet dancers were painted over and the original swagged, fringed, and tasseled curtains were removed. The stadium seating was replaced by a split-level dance floor. Airbrushed murals of the Bee Gees and other retro 1970s pop music icons found their place on the lobby walls. A later club incarnation caused the original teal, yellow, and crimson tile lining the entryway to be removed and replaced by modern green tile. Local preservationists spoke out against it to no avail. Now even the green tile is gone, covered over by blue-hued stucco. Nightclub names and themes come and go, but the Studio's exterior has largely remained. Here is a 2008 view of the original box office, one of the finest to survive from the postwar period in California. (Gary Lee Parks.)

Three

TOURING THE
CALIFORNIA THEATRE

It seems every sizeable city with numerous theatres has one regarded more fondly than any other. Such it is with the California Theatre, designed at the outset to be the South Bay's theatrical *grande dame*. Time, name and policy changes, redecorations, dark years, a postponed reawakening, and major changes in structure and layout have not diminished its status.

Opened in 1927 on a block developed by real estate magnate T. S. Montgomery, and designed by San Francisco architects Charles Peter Weeks and William Day, the new California embodied the escapist fantasy inspired by show business during the decade of the wildly eclectic 1920s. Premiering under the banner of West Coast Theatres, which had been purchased by the William Fox organization in 1925, this palatial showplace presented first-run motion pictures and live stage revues and music on the same bill. The stage attractions were the creation of brother and sister vaudeville impresarios Fanchon and Marco Wolf. These "Ideas," as they were called, revolved around a fanciful theme with such names as "California Capers Idea," "Jazz Buccaneers Idea," and "Garden of Dreams Idea," and featured the singing and dancing Sunkist Beauties chorus girls. These "Ideas" toured the Fox theatre circuits. At times, a presentation would feature a personal appearance by a star of stage or screen. In the orchestra pit were musicians to accompany both the stage attractions and the movies. In the center of the pit was the console of the mighty Wurlitzer organ.

Not long after the 1929 stock market crash, most theatres everywhere simplified their programming to save money. The California settled down to becoming chiefly a movie theatre, albeit still the most luxurious in town. Stage attractions were featured on occasion into the 1950s, and then movies reigned solely up until the theatre's commercial closure in the early 1970s. After a brief use as a rock concert hall and what many guessed to be its final closure, many years, plans, and proposals came and went until the California's gala reopening in 2004.

The California Theatre, the grandest in San Jose, stands brand new and proud at 345 South First Street in this 1927 photograph. The vertical sign has been moved from the "old" California (the former DeLuxe) which has been renamed the Mission. A facade of salmon-pink-tinted concrete features cast ornamentation in a style alternately referred to by historians as Spanish Colonial, Plateresque, or Spanish Gothic. Many sculpted faces are hidden in the ornamental design: eight lion heads, one human-ram-hybrid head, three Greco-Roman actor's masks, six maiden's heads, and four grimacing male human heads. Dozens more human and mythological faces and figures decorate the interior. Three multi-pane windows of amber glass fill a three-story ticket lobby with soft daylight. On the roof, just to the right of the flagpole, stands what appears to be a temporary electric sign, probably advertising the current attraction. *Flesh and the Devil*, released Christmas 1926, is playing, having taken four months to reach San Jose. The romantic tragedy still plays occasionally at silent film festivals today. (John C. Gordon Collection; Special Collections and Archives, San Jose State University.)

Here on opening day, April 16, 1927, a line reaches up South First Street to San Carlos Street. To the right of the theatre is a small vacant lot. Next to it is a one-story building proclaiming, "Lease Expires! Out we go May 1st!" Both lots would soon see the construction of the Mission Hotel, which would link the theatre facade stylistically with the Trinkler-Dohrman Company building. With the exception of the aforementioned one-story building, all structures in this photograph stand today and have been refurbished. The Western States Life Protection lightbulb sign doubtlessly flashed on and off, leaving the word "SAFE" spelled diagonally. In a few short years, neon would replace lightbulbs as the chief way to illuminate signs. For weeks prior, newspaper advertisements heralded the California's opening with its arrival of Hollywood stars. "Bring your Kodak—make them feel welcome," encouraged one publicity piece. Organist Irma Falvey, formerly of Oakland's Grand Lake Theatre, provided accompaniment to Billie Dove in *An Affair of the Follies*. In the early 1990s, an attempt was made to locate the film, but no print could be found. Even Billie Dove herself was unable to provide any clues. (History San Jose.)

A movie palace lobby appears pristinely new only once, and here it is. Steps of salmon marble lead to carpeted terraces bordered in tile produced by local manufacturer S&S (Solon and Schimmel) Tile. Columns are clad in warm grey-veined marble. Metal and mica light fixtures, stenciled in amber, red, and blue, cast an ancient ambience upon faux stone niches and a richly stenciled beamed ceiling. Metal stanchions, inserted into holes in the floor, hold velvet ropes for corralling patrons waiting for the next show. As with the much older Victory Theatre, potted palm trees are still in vogue as a way to bring a bit of nature into a theatre's lobby. The mezzanine promenade, visible atop the stairs at the far end, is hung with tapestries depicting scenes from classical mythology. One, titled "Jupiter et Raisin," depicted the god amid people harvesting grapes. A lingering mystery is the niche murals in the style of Italy's Etruscan civilization, which appear to be almost a stylistic afterthought. They were painted over in the mid-1940s. (John C. Gordon Collection; Special Collections and Archives, San Jose State University.)

The proscenium was painted to resemble an arch of limestone blocks. Ornamental border curtains were plush black fabric with gold detailing, along with a patterned title curtain covering the movie screen. Behind was a 31-foot-deep stage. The Wurlitzer organ console sits in the center of the orchestra pit. (John C. Gordon Collection; Special Collections and Archives, San Jose State University.)

The stage was flanked by organ chambers fronted with ornate Spanish/Moorish arched grilles. Colors included tan, blue, red, green, and gold. This photograph by Faxon Atherton appeared in the July 1927 issue of *Pacific Coast Architect*. These details, restored in 2004, appear as they did in 1927. (Steve Levin.)

The year 1934 brought Shirley Temple and Disney animation, the latter in color, to the California screen. A border of animated lightbulbs chases its way around the marquee. Theatres at this time had their own artists who hand painted signs and built displays to dress up the entrance for shows. Sometimes these nearly amounted to complete temporary lobby redecorating, while at other times they would consist of a more simple assemblage of attention-getting signs and little more, as is the case here. The cashier is almost buried in the center of a specially built fascia, which all but obscures the metal and marble box office. Photographic records of such displays show how much visual excitement could be created by some sheets of poster board, a lot of paint, perhaps some glitter and glue, photographs provided by the studios, and a lot of imagination. (Jack Tillmany.)

The year 1937 brought a new neon trapezoidal marquee to the California. This design appeared on several theatres in the chain. One on the Fox in Salinas still survives, although without its decorative neon borders. The outer and grand lobbies were given new pastel color schemes. Walls were painted cream, and antique gold accents flecked the sculpted detailing. The stenciled ceiling of the ticket lobby was painted over in pink, and aqua accents appeared elsewhere. The original carpet, with its pattern of rampant lions and shields in red, blue, gold, and black, was replaced with a similarly colored pattern of an interwoven garland design. The 1,848-seat palace continued to be, as Fox West Coast always said, "The Place to Go!" This 1942 photograph was taken by Ted Newman, who did not take pictures inside, so far as is known. (Steve Levin.)

Touring theatre pianist and pioneering movie palace photographer Terry Helgesen took the next six views of the California in 1945. Here war bonds are advertised as prominently as the comedy, *Murder He Says*, and the spooky thriller, *The Unseen*. Ushers dreaded being stationed in the lobby, where the delicious smells coming from the California Bakery next door were a constant temptation. (Terry Helgesen Collection; Theatre Historical Society of America.)

Patrons step up to the original marble-clad box office. The ticket lobby floor is fashioned of small rectangular tiles of lavender and blue-grey. The 1927 poster cases have been replaced by moderne frames. The box office had been modernized by the time it was removed around 1979. Today terra-cotta tile paves this area. (Terry Helgesen Collection; Theatre Historical Society of America.)

Back toward the entrance, the lobby's pastel color scheme is evident. Also noteworthy are the multi-pane arched windows, which provided a view out through a vestibule to the ticket lobby. They have been painted over to conform to wartime blackout requirements. (Terry Helgesen Collection; Theatre Historical Society of America.)

In the grand lobby, the routes to the auditorium were made clear. Patrons could access the orchestra floor by taking stairs down through the low arch on the right or ascend a staircase to the vaulted mezzanine promenade and turn right toward the balcony. (Terry Helgesen Collection; Theatre Historical Society of America.)

The mezzanine promenade provided access to both balcony and restrooms. Throne chairs and thickly upholstered sofas made for a nice place to socialize. At the far end was a second stairway. The archway led to a balcony staircase on the right and to the theatre offices and district manager's office on the left. (Terry Helgesen Collection; Theatre Historical Society of America.)

In this final photograph from Terry Helgesen's camera, the auditorium is viewed from the higher-priced loge section at the front of the balcony. The Wurlitzer organ console is covered with protective fabric, and one of two Baldwin baby grand pianos sits in the pit. (Terry Helgesen Collection; Theatre Historical Society of America.)

Theatres were always coming up with little extras to please patrons and ultimately pay profits. Here an usherette stands ready in the grand lobby to present a corsage to the next mother entering the California as a special guest of the president of Fox West Coast. (History San Jose.)

Although vaudeville and the Fanchon and Marco "Ideas" were long gone by 1953, the stage was still used. Here dancing teacher Dorice Andreucetti and her class greet the public. For a time, she would have her class perform every Saturday afternoon at the California. The Wurlitzer organ provided accompaniment. (History San Jose.)

Later in 1953, the Wurlitzer organ was sold and removed, and a wide Cinemascope screen made its debut with the South Bay premiere of *The Egyptian*. In 1957, a new outer lobby, marquee, and sign proclaimed the theatre's new name: Fox. This photograph was taken when *Not of This Earth* was the attraction. (History San Jose.)

The lobby was given red walls with beige trim. Plastic plants, up-lit by green cove lighting, filled the niches where Etruscan figures had cavorted in 1927. Nearly the whole right side of the grand lobby was filled by a concession counter. This photograph was probably taken in 1966 when *Fantastic Voyage* was coming soon. Removal of the wall fixtures had made the lobby rather dark. (History San Jose.)

This 1970s photograph shows the 1957 Fox vertical sign and marquee. The formerly salmon-tinted facade had been painted aqua. In the 1960s, sculpted urns, lion heads, and shields were removed from the top and a coat of white paint was applied. The Mission Hotel, to the right of the Fox, would soon burn down, but Mac's bar and Sal and Luigi's Pizza would last into the 1990s. (Shirlie Montgomery; History San Jose.)

Its use as a rock concert venue in 1973 brought noteworthy performers such as the Doobie Brothers, the Steve Miller Band, Elvin Bishop, and Van Morrison, but audiences were not kind to the building. Here tattered seats look out across a dingy auditorium, where the bottom border of the "fireproof asbestos curtain" is visible at the top of the proscenium. (History San Jose.)

When the lights were turned up, the Fox's timeless beauty was still visible. But a theatre whose lobby had snacks for sale on one side and drug paraphernalia on the other side, and where drug peddlers walked the balcony calling out "buds!," did not ingratiate itself with local officials. Attempts were also made to make the Fox look more hip. Three murals were begun, two on the mezzanine and one in the orchestra level lobby. One depicted clouds surrounding the Warner Brothers WB logo, a strange accent in a theatre never affiliated with that company or its theatre chain. The other two were typical examples of the diluted surrealism of the decade. None of the murals were completed before the brief rock experiment at the Fox was brought to a halt. (Steve Levin.)

Following a concert where a riot developed because more tickets had been sold than there were seats, the Fox's public assembly permit was revoked, and the theatre closed. In the late 1970s, Jose Borges, operator of the Mexico Theatre (the former Liberty), began a renovation project to revive the Fox as a showcase for live acts and movies from Mexico. A very ambitious cosmetic restoration was begun. Some of the renovation techniques were controversial at best, such as chaining a car to the 1957 dropped ceiling late at night and attempting to pull the ceiling down with one violent wrench. The ticket lobby's original height was revealed, however. On a more refined note, the auditorium underwent a meticulous repainting. Some areas were restored as originally designed, whereas other surfaces were heavily embellished. The project ran into financial hurdles and stalled. (Steve Levin.)

The Redevelopment Agency of San Jose bought the Fox in 1985 with an eye toward ultimate revival. The theatre was made safe and secure, and various proposals for its reuse were made throughout the 1990s. Here demolition of the adjacent Sainte Claire Hotel parking garage in 2001 reveals the 1957 painted sign on the auditorium sidewall. (Gary Lee Parks.)

Finally, with Opera San Jose, Symphony Silicon Valley, and other arts groups identified as users, the Redevelopment Agency, with additional funding from the Packard Humanities Institute, began a project to expand the theatre while restoring its public spaces. Here, in 2003, removal of the 1957 marquee permitted a rare view of the facade as missing decorative elements were being replaced. (Gary Lee Parks.)

In this 2008 photograph, the California still carries its 345 South First Street address. An exact replica of the vertical sign was fashioned after an original on the California Theatre in Dunsmuir. A replica of the marquee was designed from early photographs. Missing finials, shields, and lion heads were re-created. The new stage house rises beyond. (Gary Lee Parks.)

On the Market Street side of the theatre, a new entrance and marquee were built where none had existed. Rehearsal rooms, lobby space, display windows, and a loading dock for the new stage occupy this addition to the theatre. The 1926 Sainte Claire Hotel, also the work of California architects Weeks and Day, backs up against the stage house. (Gary Lee Parks.)

Except for the missing box office, the ticket lobby of the California faithfully replicates, as closely as possible, what moviegoers saw when they first entered the theatre in 1927. Poster cases along the north wall serve as the windows of a new ticket office. Light fixtures have been replicated from photographs. Mirrored false balconies once again wear their wood-grain finishes. The walls are painted to imitate blocks of limestone, as they were originally. The ceiling bears stenciling in deep crimson, blue, and antique gold. Mahogany doors, topped with wrought-metal ornament, duplicate what was once there, and arched multi-pane windows let light through the vestibule to the grand lobby for the first time since World War II. Once in the grand lobby, patrons are sometimes treated to music from a small Wurlitzer organ, placed in chambers beneath the floor and played from a console situated where the concession counter once was. (Gary Lee Parks.)

The California is shown here soon after its 2004 gala reopening. The first program, an Opera San Jose production of *The Marriage of Figaro*, is on the marquee. Although the additions to the theatre behind the scenes and beyond the boundaries of the original building are contemporary in style, careful attention was paid to keep the historic public spaces visually separate from the modern ones. The seating capacity is now 1,146, reflecting a need for wider seats and added legroom. The new orchestra pit can raise and lower a full compliment of musicians, as well as the console of the 4-manual, 21-rank Wurlitzer organ. The organ sometimes joins orchestras onstage and at other times serenades film festival audiences and reprises its original role as the giver of voices to the silent screen. In the lobby is another, smaller Wurlitzer. Both instruments are owned by the Packard Humanities Institute and are restored and maintained by Edward Millington Stout III and Dick Taylor. San Jose's grandest theatre is still "The Place to Go!" (Martin Schmidt.)

Four

THE NEIGHBORHOOD THEATRES

Clustered around downtown San Jose, a ring of neighborhoods provides grace and charm. Some established themselves organically with individual houses built one by one. Others stand as early examples of planned development; in these neighborhoods can be found Queen Anne Victorians, Craftsman bungalows, Spanish Colonial cottages, and other examples of domestic design from the first half of the 20th century. These houses, combined with tree-lined streets and a sense of place and permanence, make these neighborhoods highly desirable places to live even now. In addition, each has at least one primary commercial street.

Naturally, as these neighborhoods thrived, theatres were a logical addition. Starting in the mid-1920s with the Hester in the neighborhood of the same name, a pattern of building theatres beyond the edge of downtown commenced. This continued with the growth of the suburbs after World War II and has extended into the movie multiplex and megaplex era of the 21st century. As long as San Jose continues to grow and there are movies to show, neighborhood theatres will be there. This chapter chronicles the beginnings of that trend.

Binder and Curtis designed the Hester Theatre at 1433 The Alameda for Victor A. Benson on the site of his garage. Leased by Enno Lion and E. Rosenthal, it was to have seated over 1,000 and is said to have been Egyptian in style throughout. As built, it seated slightly fewer. This photograph shows a simple Spanish-style facade, eyewitness accounts of its interior prior to 1952 confirm a Spanish theme, and the proscenium arch that remains today is Spanish. Newspapers reported that the theatre was completely redecorated in 1930, so perhaps there was indeed an earlier Egyptian design up until that point. Someday possibly, some urban archaeologist examining the building behind the walls and above the ceilings may find fragmentary evidence of Pharaoh's influence. In a 1942 Ted Newman photograph, a new neon marquee adorns this, San Jose's first neighborhood theatre. (Steve Levin.)

From its 1925 opening, a small pipe organ accompanied silent movies until sound was installed in 1930. Its console was squeezed into a tiny orchestra pit, which could also hold a few musicians. A small stage could be used for live acts. In this 1986 view, its 1952 facade and name, Towne, still catch the eye. The marquee was really an enlargement of the one shown in the preceding photograph. The stylized floral sculpture above it featured pink and green animated neon glowing from behind. Adult movies were the fare in the 1970s and 1980s. *Fashion Fantasies* revolved around a "magic" dress supposedly worn by Mae West, and the less said about the second feature, perhaps, the better. (Gary Lee Parks.)

In the late 1980s, San Jose passed legislation banning all adult entertainment businesses from operating within 500 yards of a school. Hester Elementary School is located across the street from the theatre. When Pussycat Theatres left the scene as a result of this ruling, Camera Cinemas arrived in 1990 and began exhibiting foreign and independent film fare. A large Wurlitzer organ, originally housed in Chicago's State Lake Theatre and which later spent most of the 1960s and 1970s playing for classic movie fans in San Francisco's Avenue Theatre, was installed behind the screen of the Towne. Its console was barely shoehorned into the original orchestra pit. Sunday afternoon concerts and silent movies were presented. The auditorium was tripled. While this softened the acoustic effect of the organ, it enabled the theatre to survive. A decade later, with the opening of the Camera 12 downtown, the Towne switched to a diet of films from India. (Martin Schmidt.)

March 4, 1933, saw Santa Clara County get its first theatre built after the advent of talking pictures. Another design by Binder and Curtis, the 475-seat house was the brainchild of D. L. McKay and manager Milton Samis. The entrance of the theatre as built had no marquee. Rather a little arcade of three arches gave the front a sedate, little Spanish town flavor. In this 1944 Ted Newman photograph, 1184 Lincoln Avenue has had a face-lift. The triple-arched entrance has been replaced by a streamlined neon marquee, which was joined to the original vertical sign. (Steve Levin.)

A staff of usherettes, led by hostess Rosalie Borroughs, wore wide-brimmed hats, peasant tops with embroidered vests, and calf-length full skirts coordinating with the Spanish or Mexican style of the theatre when it opened. The year 1944 saw the Willow Glen wearing its first decade well. A color scheme of cream, gold, and assorted pastel accents was used throughout the interior. The silver-grey satin curtain was washed with multicolored light. (Steve Levin.)

The decorated panels at the rear were balsam wood covered with fabric, absorbing 56 percent of the echo from the RCA High Fidelity sound system. In 1949, with the opening of the Garden Theatre up the street, the Willow Glen became the Vogue, presenting "artistic, foreign language, and classic films." Unable to compete with its palatial new neighbor, the Vogue soon closed. The building has housed a thrift store for many years. (Steve Levin.)

At the southwest corner of Bascom Avenue and Stevens Creek Boulevard stands a quarter-circle strip mall, best known for the Time Delicatessen with its big neon clock. Originally, this center was to have had a theatre in its middle, and the above rendering shows how the design by Otto A. Deichmann would have appeared. Instead, the name Garden would appear on a new theatre for the Willow Glen neighborhood. (Steve Levin.)

Using plans drawn up by architect Deichmann for a theatre originally planned for East San Jose, exhibitors Jimmy Lima, Ben Levin, and Walter Preddy opened the 1,000-seat Garden Theatre on June 22, 1949. Theatres were often barely ready in time. Here neon borders on the marquee have yet to be lit. Neon spelled out the name in green and magenta, while leaves of green and yellow animated rapidly. (Steve Levin.)

A smartly modern entry of turquoise and yellow tile with a pavement of green, yellow, and red terrazzo invited patrons toward the etched-glass doors. All of these areas took the theatre's name as their inspiration. Leaves curved across the pavement, where large blossoms echoed the blinking neon blossom at the top of the vertical sign. Leaves filled the door panels and bordered the box office window panes. Moviegoers on that first night saw the film noir tale of slum life *Knock on Any Door* paired with a feel-good Disney live action offering, *So Dear to My Heart* starring Burl Ives. (Steve Levin.)

Obviously proud of their new theatre, owners Ben Levin (left) and Jimmy Lima (right) pose by the tile and etched-glass box office. Two other Bay Area theatres used this exact box office design: Gilroy's Strand and Menlo Park's Park. The Garden would remain architecturally unchanged for its entire run as a theatre. (Steve Levin.)

The lobby of the Garden was pure streamline. A floral-patterned carpet gave a nod to the theatre's name. Sculpted panels behind the concession counter depicted a bear, salmon, hare, and a gnawing beaver. These panels, part of an interior artistic scheme by Anthony Heinsbergen, also appear in his Fourth Avenue Theatre in Anchorage, Alaska. Heinsbergen had decorated the interior of the California Theatre downtown over 20 years earlier. (Steve Levin.)

In the auditorium, the plain grey ceiling was balanced by crimson walls. On the left, a mural celebrated the valley's agricultural bounty, while a mural on the right paid homage to San Jose's industrial prowess. The human figures were painted in oils on silhouettes of canvas that were glued to the walls. The surrounding details were painted directly onto the textured acoustical stucco. The curtain and screen were flanked by murals of paired maidens and a dancing couple set against enormous flowers. (Steve Levin.)

Six brass-colored chandeliers hung from saucer-shaped air vents. This photograph is proof that the stadium seating so popular in today's cinemas is by no means a new idea. Many theatres as far back as the 1920s were built this way, both for good sight lines and as an efficient use of space. Very often, as at the Garden, the lobby, lounge, and restrooms could fit perfectly under a stadium section. (Steve Levin.)

There were two philosophies about double features then. One was to pair films of similar genre. The other was to pair films of two different types, in a "something for everyone" approach. With the comedy *Mr. Belvedere Goes to College* sharing the screen with Maria Montez as Queen Antinea, the Garden was subscribing to the second approach. (Steve Levin.)

"He's the man, the man with the Midas touch"—so go the undulating vocals of Shirley Bassey in the *Goldfinger* theme. Indeed, the box office did strike gold with this James Bond picture in 1964, paired with a revival of 1962's *Dr. No*. A record store and an optometrist operate out of the two small retail spaces on either side of the theatre entrance. (Steve Levin.)

In 1975, the Garden was sold to an exhibitor of Spanish-language films. The theatre closed in 1988. Camera Cinemas expressed interest in buying it for art theatre use, perhaps as a triplex, but the asking price was too high, so they opted for the Towne Theatre instead. Pictured here in 1989, the Garden was about to be gutted and turned into office and retail space. (Gary Lee Parks.)

Elements of the Garden's interior were salvaged by East Bay movie exhibitor Allen Michaan, and some parts reappeared in theatres operated by him. The mural figures on either side of the screen now cavort inside a subsidiary cinema added to the Orinda Theatre. Several of the etched-glass doors (detail shown at right) find use in the Orinda and in the Oaks Theatre in Berkeley. (Gary Lee Parks.)

Here is the exterior of the Garden in 2008. Most of the neon is gone from the marquee, but the vertical sign's tubing, very recently refurbished, still animates. Poster cases to the left of the entrance now serve as windows into a coffee shop, where photographs of the Garden's life as a theatre are on display. Behind the building, the long, narrow parking lot now serves shoppers and diners, where once the autos of moviegoers filled the spaces. (Gary Lee Parks.)

The Mayfair Theatre opened at 1194 East Santa Clara Street on May 20, 1949. The first movie was *Red River* with John Wayne. A 1949 Buick was given away. An advertisement for the theatre boasted "lounging luxury" seating: "Every seat a loge." A glassed-in soundproof seating area for parents with fussing infants was provided. Renamed Esquire in 1962, it became the Mexico nearly 20 years later. (Jack Tillmany.)

The signs on the marquee were removed from the "old" Mexico (former Liberty) when that downtown theatre closed, but the former Mayfair's neon continued to glow as always. *Abierto Dia y Noche* and *El Dia del Compadre*, both comedies with Jorge Rivero, were released in 1981 and 1983, respectively. (Gary Lee Parks.)

In the mid-1990s, a policy of Asian films was tried at the Mexico. In 2002, the theatre was in use as a church. By 2004, it stood vacant. Recently, a few proposals for adaptive reuse have surfaced, including conversion to a tropical fish store. There has been some local advocacy for making sure that the exterior is preserved, but at present, nothing seems certain. (Jack Tillmany.)

The 930-seat Burbank, at 552 Bascom Avenue, opened September 5, 1951, with a double feature of *On Moonlight Bay* with Doris Day and Gordon MacRae and *Gunplay*, a Western starring Tim Holt. Once again, father and son Alexander and McKenzie Cantin were at the architectural helm of a new San Jose Theatre. (Steve Levin.)

The Burbank's neon glows faintly against a threatening sky in this 1990 photograph. The Burbank was not the big success it was hoped to be. It closed in July 1955. The owners of the Crest, Garden, Jose, and Liberty purchased it a few months later. In 1964, it was leased to Mason Shaw, who began an art film policy, which would not compete with the aforementioned theatres. "Cinema," in mint-green neon script, was added to the marquee at this time. In 1973, Shaw Theatres subleased it to an adult film operation, which continued until 1977. That year, Pat and Vi Moore, having been very successful with a policy of classic movies at the Saratoga Theatre on Big Basin Way, sought to run an identical operation at the Burbank. This was not a success, and the Moores retreated to Saratoga, where their beloved Vitaphone Saratoga operation would live on into the 1980s. Porn returned in 1978, and the marquee carried the message pictured above until the theatre's closure in 2000. (Gary Lee Parks.)

And so began a period of closure that has yet to resolve. An unfinished grey and blue paint job, which stopped far short of fully covering the pink and mustard tones on the marquee, gave the Burbank a shabby, patchwork appearance from the late 1980s on. The stucco exterior had formerly been mint, which harmonized with the tile and terrazzo entry, seen here in these two photographs from 2000. (Gary Lee Parks.)

The crucial factor that works against the Burbank's revival is lack of parking. After so many years of the sporadic and discrete arrivals and departures of X-rated movie patrons, local residents are no longer used to the added traffic that a full-time movie or live entertainment policy might bring to the theatre. This, and the costs involved in refurbishing the Burbank, has thus far thwarted all plans. (Gary Lee Parks.)

Five

AROUND THE VALLEY

As San Jose's theatres were opening to the throngs who were hungry for entertainment, showmen of perhaps lesser renown but identical determination brought stage and screen delights to the inhabitants of the other cities and towns that dotted the Santa Clara Valley surrounding the central metropolis. This made complete sense, as it was then a long trek from each of these communities to San Jose itself. If one were to see a show in the evening in San Jose, arrival back home in Los Gatos or Sunnyvale would be late indeed. Roads were far fewer and often made of dirt, and the Interurban Railway lines, while efficient for the day, still took time.

As with San Jose itself, the earliest entertainment was presented in whatever meeting halls were available. Soon each city or town had its own theatre for stage and screen presentations. In some instances, more than one theatre was in operation at a given time, but in most cases, a single theatre was all a community needed. After World War II, when the orchards began to give way to the suburbs, which would ultimately join together all of the valley's cities and towns seamlessly, newer theatres and drive-ins sprung up. In most cases, this meant the ultimate demise of the original Main Street theatres. Only one of these, the Los Gatos, still operates today as a full-time motion picture venue. It remains the oldest continuously operating movie theatre in Santa Clara County.

If one were to stand today in downtown Campbell in the same spot where this 1924 photograph was taken, the similarities would be striking. The road surface and the street furniture are different, but the buildings have changed very little, and even the majestic tree still welcomes visitors to this quaint stretch of Campbell Avenue. In the first building on the left can be seen the entrance to the Orchard City Theatre, which opened in September 1920 for movies with live or player piano accompaniment. In December 1924, a $3,000 Wurlitzer organ was installed. Sound movies came in November 1931 when the theatre was renamed the Campbell. The building's white glazed-brick exterior appears exactly the same today, but all interior traces of the theatre are gone. Two doors up can be seen the taller front of the Growers National Bank building. In May 1939, the vacated bank opened as the "new" Campbell Theatre. (Jack Tillmany.)

Here in a 1980s photograph is the Campbell Theatre, renamed the Gaslighter but otherwise unchanged from its movie days, on the outside at least. It was operated by Blanco's Peninsular Theatres, along with the Sunnyvale, the Mountain View, and the Cinema in Mountain View. In 1953, the Campbell closed because of the popularity of television and drive-ins. Reopening in 1960 with a much larger screen, it still had trouble, opening and closing throughout the decade until 1966. Don and Faye Cupp purchased the theatre in 1968 and began presenting live 19th-century-style melodrama. In 1980, pianist Mark Gaetano bought the house, and its popularity continued. Audiences would cheer the hero and boo the villain, and popcorn was thrown as often as it was eaten. Plays with names like *Angel of Alviso Slough*, *Dirty Deeds at Dry Diggin's*, and *The Perrils* [sic] *of Sweet Polly Dimple* shared the bill with vaudeville acts. The theatre closed around 2005. Today both former theatres on Campbell Avenue sit vacant. (Jack Tillmany.)

Here in this 1904 scene of Main Street viewed from Montebello Way, Los Gatos appears to be experiencing a building boom. The dark, imposing structure in the center is Ford's Opera House, which opened in October of that year. The 500-seat theatre was built over a pair of retail spaces that shared the frontage with the theatre entrance in the center. (Los Gatos Public Library.)

Ford's Opera House stands complete in this postcard view. In the foreground can be seen a railroad crossing guard in the up position. The railroad line continued all the way through the mountains to drop passengers off in front of the Santa Cruz Casino, Plunge, and Boardwalk. The building on the corner at the left is an early example of the California Mission Revival style, which was beginning to sweep the state. The two-story building in the distance is the still-standing Montezuma Block, which briefly housed a storefront nickelodeon. (Los Gatos Public Library.)

The auditorium of Ford's Opera House was completely clad in pressed-metal ornamental panels. The proscenium arch, walls, ceiling, and balcony front were outfitted with these catalog-order elements. In addition to the chandeliers, close inspection of this photograph reveals bare lightbulbs spaced across the ceiling and the arch. Advertising space could be rented on the curtain. Some of the merchants include A. M. Bogart Hardware, H. S. Beckworth Groceries, Gem City Garage, and Park Café and Lunch Counter (25¢ lunch!). Two drugstores vie for patrons, as do two more grocers, and O. J. Lewis and Son Hardware has the advantage of carrying Sherwin-Williams paint. These scenic advertising curtains, which often doubled as fire curtains, were frequently used to great advantage by traveling comedians, who would glance at a merchant's name advertised thereon and tailor their monologue accordingly, as in, "So this morning I was walking down Santa Cruz Avenue, and what do I see walking out of Beckwith's Grocery store, but a man with a chicken on his head! I said to him . . ." (Los Gatos Public Library.)

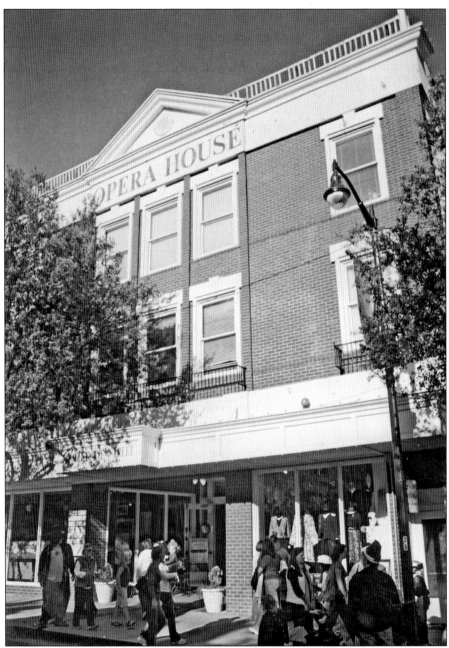

In 1916, the opera house was converted to a department store. A tastefully ornamental Spanish Colonial facade was added to it. The pressed-tin walls and ceiling of the auditorium were largely left alone. Years later, the Spanish-style exterior was stripped, to be replaced by a simple moderne stucco look. This caused a number of visitors over the years to wonder if the building had once been a movie theatre. A project to return the facade to its original 1904 appearance was underway when the 1989 Loma Prieta earthquake struck. Delayed but undeterred, the project was completed. Retail stores flourish at street level, and upstairs the former auditorium is available for weddings and other private functions. Sections of the original pressed tin have been preserved as part of the decor. (Gary Lee Parks.)

There were earlier movie theatres in Los Gatos: the Feature, the Photoplay, and the "old" Los Gatos. The Los Gatos closed when the Strand (shown above) opened on November 16, 1916, at 41 North Santa Cruz Avenue, with a row of five commercial spaces to its left, together known as the Marshall Building. Buell Walbridge conducted the Strand Orchestra. Helen Walbridge was at the piano. Three short subjects and a feature, *The Chattel*, were on the opening bill. (Los Gatos Library.)

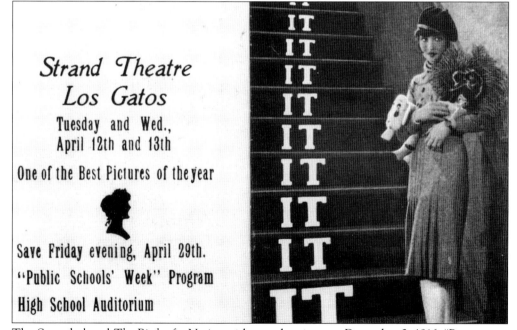

The Strand played *The Birth of a Nation* with two showings on December 2, 1916. "Promptness at the appointed hour is desirable," proclaimed the newspaper. In the above 1920s advertisement, Clara Bow is appearing in her signature movie, *IT*. It was not unusual during these years for a theatre to change shows daily. One must remember that movies were being made in enormous quantities, and the majority have not survived. *IT*, however, still enjoys screenings at silent film festivals. (Chuck Bergtold; Los Gatos Public Library.)

Santa Cruz Ave.—looking south Los Gatos, Calif.

Following a 1929 fire, the theatre was refurbished and given a new name, the Premier. Louis Zelinski was the new manager. The ticket lobby received new walls covered in black, red, and green Moorish-patterned tiles. As if a fire were not enough, in 1933, a bomb went off in the ticket office. Debris flew 50 feet into the street. Such a box office bombing was not unusual. A similar bomb was planted at San Francisco's Alhambra Theatre, but it did not explode. These demonstrations of unrest were due to labor disputes. The coming of talking pictures, together with the onset of the Depression, resulted in widespread firings of theatre musicians, who did not usually take such a turn of events lightly. Today many of the buildings in this photograph remain. The street is narrower because of added plantings and benches. The cleaners, druggist, 5-10-15¢ store, hardware store, and mom-and-pop restaurants have been replaced by high-fashion boutiques, jewelers, home decor specialists, and themed eateries. (Los Gatos Public Library.)

Theatre tickets, if not actually saved, are known to be lost in the nooks and crannies of a theatre. These examples from the Premier have not been torn. Despite so many different computerized methods of ticketing today, numbered tickets of this type are still manufactured. Many independent movie theatres still use them today, as do fairs, carnivals, and raffles. (Chuck Bergtold; Los Gatos Public Library.)

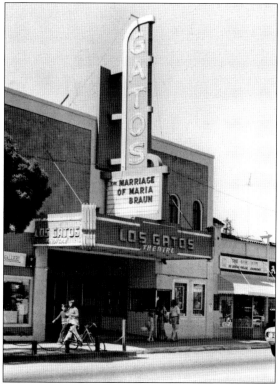

In 1941, the Premier became the Los Gatos. All of the original ornament was removed from the façade, and a new marquee and vertical sign took center stage. Murals of maidens pouring water from urns were painted on the walls flanking the screen. In 1975, the Los Gatos was bought by Carmel Cormack. She ran the theatre and lived in the apartment over the entrance. (Jack Tillmany.)

Following the 1989 earthquake, conversion of the Los Gatos Theatre into a collection of shops was considered. Instead, seismic retrofitting was undertaken, and the theatre was twinned crosswise. The original proscenium remained in the forward part of the auditorium, and the second screen occupied the rear half. Original ornamental plaster from 1916 was hidden behind the red fabric of the auditorium sidewalls. The first operator following the remodeling was unsuccessful. Screens seemed too large and close to the front rows of seating. Exit signs, while mandatory, glared vivid green and distracted from the movies. The murals of maidens were covered with the uniform red wall curtains. Camera Cinemas stepped-in, made some much-needed technical and audience comfort improvements, uncovered the murals, and have maintained a cozy and friendly atmosphere at this, the Santa Clara Valley's oldest operating full-time movie theatre. (Martin Schmidt.)

Following World War II, all-metal Quonset huts, developed for military construction in 1941, became available for peacetime use in large numbers. Their use for theatres became widespread. One such theatre was the Saratoga, opening in 1947 at Third Street and Big Basin Way. In this photograph, the corrugated Quonset hut can be seen to the rear of the lobby and retail structure fronting Big Basin Way. (Saratoga Historical Museum.)

The 400-seat theatre was first operated by Mason Shaw. In 1974, Pat and Vi Moore began a classic film policy, the "Vitaphone Saratoga." Pat would talk about the evening's films. Cobbler and ice cream were served as well as more typical concessions. The Moores' cat was fed down front, to the delight of the audience. This 1982 photograph shows the Saratoga soon before its closure and subsequent demolition. (Gary Lee Parks.)

The City of Santa Clara once had its own downtown, which largely vanished during the nationwide urban renewal schemes of the 1960s. An early theatre, the Franklin, had this scenic advertising curtain, much like that of Ford's Opera House in Los Gatos. All traces of this theatre vanished decades ago, along with much of Franklin Street, from which its name derived. (History San Jose.)

This theatre, which opened in 1925 at 966 Franklin Street, was originally the Casa Grande. Appropriately, architects Binder and Curtis gave it a rambling Spanish Colonial look, with tile-roofed retail wings flanking the theatre entrance. The Casa Grande was operated by Peter Kyprious and John Vasconcellas. It is shown here in 1939, when it reopened with a new facade and name, the Santa Clara. (John C. Gordon Collection; Special Collections and Archives, San Jose State University.)

In this 1942 photograph by insurance photographer Ted Newman, Santa Clara Building and Loan occupies the storefront on the left, and Genova Delicatessen is on the right. A romantic Western, *The Great Man's Lady*, stars Barbara Stanwyck and Joel McCrea, and *Confessions of Boston Blackie*, with Chester Morris, involved complications beginning with a murder at an art auction. (Steve Levin.)

In 1960, the best film entertainment still came to the Santa Clara. Marilyn Monroe starred with Yves Montand and Tony Randall in *Let's Make Love*. *When Comedy Was King* was a documentary about the great silent movie comic actors of an era that had ended over three decades before. Genova Delicatessen was still serving sandwiches, but a watch repair shop had replaced Santa Clara Building and Loan. (The City of Santa Clara History Collection.)

This 1960s view shows the left retail wing that was part of the theatre building. Above the tiled roofs can be seen the concrete structure of the auditorium, which resembles that of the Hester (Towne) Theatre, also by Binder and Curtis. Santa Clara Cyclery, University Smoke Shop, Downing's Furniture, and that little watch and clock repair shop are the tenants. All would be demolished later in the decade. (The City of Santa Clara History Collection.)

Though also hit hard by urban renewal, Sunnyvale's downtown preserved one block of Murphy Avenue. Both early theatres stood on that block. The first, the Strand, was a nickelodeon-style affair. It shared frontage with a drugstore, as seen in this c. 1915 holiday parade photograph. A movie with screen siren Pola Negri is the attraction. (Sunnyvale Historical Society and Museum Association.)

The "new" Strand Theatre opened around 1926 at 146–148 South Murphy Avenue right next to the structure housing the "old" Strand. Exhibiting five different shows a week, and equipped with an organ and small stage, it was quite a fine showplace for this agricultural community. The 1927 schedule shows a nearly movies-only policy, but small musical acts did perform, and Oreol McLaughlin of Our Gang Comedies made a personal appearance. At that time, adult admission was 30¢; children were 15¢, and anyone sitting in the loge section paid 40¢. After it was renamed the Sunnyvale in 1935, Blanco's Peninsular Theatres took over operation from 1937 to 1943. The theatre seated 934 in a stadium-style arrangement. There was an upstairs lounge where a pair of arched windows of textured glass presented a view out over the marquee. Perhaps this postman was looking forward to the "Two Good Pictures Tonite" advertised thereon after completing his route. (Sunnyvale Historical Society and Museum Association.)

A wider and more workaday Murphy Avenue than exists today is shown in this view from the 1950s. Most of the buildings still stand, however. The remarkably tall neon vertical sign of the Sunnyvale Theatre would have been noticeable all the way from El Camino Real. Sign and marquee were painted red, yellow, and white at this time. (Sunnyvale Historical Society and Museum.)

In the early 1960s, with the nearby opening of the Town and Country shopping center, the Sunnyvale received a drastic remodeling and was renamed Town and Country Cinema. The "old" Strand was where the El Nuevo Curimeo bar is located in this 1980s photograph. Compare the cornice at the top of the building with the photograph on page 114. Fibbar MaGee's Irish pub is there now. (Sunnyvale Historical Society and Museum Association.)

After several years of showing X-rated fare, a mid-1980s film policy of two, three, or even four features kept the lights on at the renamed Murphy Avenue Cinema. A six-week repertory calendar was distributed locally, and *The Rocky Horror Picture Show* did what only it can do on Saturdays at midnight. Here a modern projector sits in the original 1920s booth. (Sunnyvale Historical Society and Museum Association.)

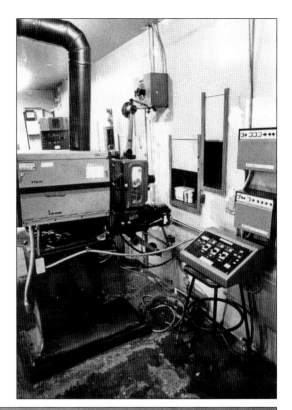

In the late 1980s, a group of entrepreneurs began a complete remodeling of the theatre with the intent of opening a "dinner and movie" beer and pizza pub operation, an idea proliferating elsewhere. The theatre did not reopen. This 1990 photograph shows how the original 1920s windows had been uncovered and a neo-moderne facade had been designed. (Gary Lee Parks.)

The theatre did finally find new life, but not with movies. The interior was given an elaborate remodeling with terraces for dining built in the former stadium seating area. A dance floor and stage were built down front. Egyptian-derived columns and free-form curving shapes decorated the sidewalls. Later updates included a Romano-Tuscan theme, in which statues and gilt-framed mirrors graced the lobby and painted sphinxes appeared on the exterior. Functioning variously since the mid-1990s as a nightclub, restaurant, and meeting facility under such names as Palace, Forum, and Abyss, it is yet alive. Through it all, this red, yellow, and green terrazzo sidewalk still bears witness underfoot that once, a theatre flourished here. As of 2008, Sunnyvale is without a movie theatre, although a multiplex is planned for the new development on the site of the demolished Town Center mall, two blocks south.

Six

DOMES AND STARLIGHT

Theatres that opened soon after World War II did so under the assumption that movies would be keeping their decades-long status as America's main form of cheap entertainment. Television was at first a technological curiosity and then became a serious contender for the public's attention. Multitudes stayed at home to watch television, and the movie theatre business would never be the same.

By the 1960s, many downtown movie palaces across America were closing and being demolished. Drive-in theatres now proliferated in suburbs and rural areas. They were popular for whole families and especially for young people who were raised with America's pervasive car culture.

There was still a market for new indoor movie theatres. They too found their place in the suburbs. They were modernistic tributes to the world of tomorrow. This was as potent a fantasy as that of the opulent showplaces of years earlier. Once again, skilled architects made use of the styles of the day. The main attraction, however, was presentation technology. The theatres themselves were very comfortable, but the main amenities promoted by the exhibitors were the wide screens, superior sound and projection, and clarity of image and color, which television could never hope to match. This, however, was the last mighty gasp of traditional movie showmanship prior to the multiplex era.

Of all the drive-ins built in San Jose, only one, the Capitol, survives. The domed Century Theatres, with their architectural futurism, are now looked upon by moviegoers with perhaps as much nostalgia as older generations have had for the movie palaces of downtown.

Despite being a hub of such sweeping cultural and technological change, the Santa Clara Valley has made significant strides in preserving its history. Many of its theatres live on only in photographs, but a few, including some of the best, still stand, having their valued place in today's San Jose.

Raymond Syufy and his family had been in movie exhibition since the 1940s. The association of the Syufy theatres with architect Vincent G. Raney dated back to that decade as well. The Century 21 dome was a departure for both exhibitor and architect and was an iconic symbol of things to come. Originally planned as a showplace for the three-projector Cinerama process, it opened without it but did exhibit 70-mm presentations. (Jack Tillmany.)

The Century 21, opening in 1964 at 3161 Olsen Drive, was a tremendous success. The movie *2001: A Space Odyssey* ran longer there than at any other theatre. Century 22 (shown here with two smaller domes added in the 1970s) opened at 3162 Olin Avenue in 1966. Architect Raney would keep designing theatres for Century into the early 1990s. (Jack Tillmany.)

The Boulevard Domes, as they came to be called, continued to rise. The Century 23, at 3164 Olsen Drive, opened in March 1968. Another dome, Century 24, opened beyond the 280 freeway at 741 South Winchester Boulevard in 1968. (Jack Tillmany.)

In this 1989 photograph, the sign pylon shared by the first three Century theatres bears a proclamation of the Century 21's 25th anniversary. In the intervening years, Century domes had been built in Oakland, Pleasant Hill, and Sacramento. Other domes appeared as far away as Anaheim and in Salt Lake City. (Jack Tillmany.)

In 1969, Century 25 opened at 1694 Saratoga Avenue. More domes, though smaller, would soon appear in South San Jose, Fremont, and Newark. Some, like the 23, 24, and 25, would be twinned or even multiplexed, just like so many of their 1920s and 1930s forebears. Vincent Raney continued to design larger cinema complexes for Century, abandoning the dome design in favor of a polygon-shaped auditorium concept. (Jack Tillmany.)

Across from the Century domes on Winchester Boulevard, competition arose. Not wanting to be left only with theatres downtown, Fox made the jump into suburbia with the Town and Country Theatre in 1966. Here in this photograph from that year, *The Blue Max*, a World War I drama starring George Peppard and James Mason, is showing. Acquired and run by Century, the Town and Country was demolished in 2001 for the Santana Row development. (History San Jose.)

The first of a series of showplaces opened by United Artists Theatre Circuit for the new Dimension 150 All-Purpose Projection System, the Cinema 150 opened in 1966 in Santa Clara's Moonlite Shopping Center on El Camino Real near the Moonlite Drive-In. Its arched lobby featured multi-globe chandeliers, and the 901-seat auditorium conveyed a feeling of understated harmony of line. El Camino Medical Group stands on the site today. (Jack Tillmany.)

Named for the mascot of San Jose State University, the Spartan Drive-In flashed its neon and chaser light sign along Monterey Highway south of downtown. In this 1965 photograph, *The Lady L* with Paul Newman and Sophia Loren is paired with *The Loved One* in which Jonathan Winters appears with an all-star cast. The Spartan closed in 1976. (Shirlie Montgomery; History San Jose.)

El Rancho Drive-In, at 1505 Almaden Road, was opened by Paul R. Catalana, who would achieve greater success in the 1960s as a promoter of rock shows. Here single-tube neon letters, vaguely reminiscent of lariat rope, and an antique wagon wheel welcome cars into the theatre, which lasted into the 1980s. The site is now occupied by housing. (Shirlie Montgomery; History San Jose.)

Paul Catalana also operated the Tropicaire Twin Vue at 1969 Alum Rock Boulevard. This was the aesthetic golden age of the tiki and torch trend and the era of the backyard Lanai. The neon palm trees tower over their living brethren by the sign pylon. Unlike some multi-screen drive-ins built later, these screens were positioned to avoid distracting patrons from the show they came to see. (Shirlie Montgomery; History San Jose.)

The Moonlite Drive-In in Santa Clara had a no-nonsense sign matching that of the Cinema 150 next to it. Released in 1966, *Glass Bottom Boat* starred Doris Day, Rod Taylor, and Arthur Godfrey. *Around the World Under the Sea*, a submarine drama starring Lloyd Bridges, did not do well at the box office. *Speed O Mania* sounds like ideal drive-in fare. (Shirley Montgomery; History San Jose.)

In their move to advance beyond the confines of downtown, Fox opened the Fox Bayshore Drive-In at First Street and Brokaw Road. Space was provided for 1,190 cars. There was a playground, and portable car heaters were available. The Garden Theatre in Willow Glen presented *Goldfinger* and *Dr. No* in a double feature in 1964, so it is likely this photograph dates from around that time. (Shirlie Montgomery; History San Jose.)

"Frontier Village, that's where the action is—the fastest fun in the West!" So began the television jingle for the beloved and greatly missed amusement park. Adjacent to it was the Frontier Auto Movie. The address was 4885 Monterey Road. Today former Frontier Village employees gather online and in person to reminisce, but the drive-in, which closed in 1974 and was demolished in 1980, is scarcely mentioned today. (Shirlie Montgomery; History San Jose.)

The Capitol Drive-In opened at 3630 Hillcap Avenue in 1971. Operated for many years by Century Theatres, which opened a multiplex next to it in the 1990s, the Capitol is now operated by West Wind Drive-Ins, a company that has kept alive the idea of the drive-in movie as a way of getting out of the house and seeing a show. (Jack Tillmany.)

BIBLIOGRAPHY

Arbuckle, Clyde. *Clyde Arbuckle's History of San Jose*. San Jose, CA: Smith and McKay Printing Company, 1985.

Boston, Linda Larson. *San Jose's Vaudeville House: Theatre Jose*. San Jose, CA: self-published, 2000.

Bowers, Q. David. *Nickelodeon Theatres and Their Music*. New York, NY: The Vestal Press, Ltd., 1986.

Douglas, Jack. *Historical Footnotes of Santa Clara Valley*. San Jose, CA: San Jose Historical Museum Association, 1993.

———. *Historical Highlights of Santa Clara Valley*. San Jose, CA: History San Jose, 2005.

Kaufmann, Preston J. *Fox, The Last Word . . . Story of the World's Finest Theatre*. Pasadena, CA: Showcase Publications, 1979.

Marquee. The Journal of the Theatre Historical Society of America, especially Vol. 27 No. 4, Vol. 33 No. 4, and Vol. 39 No. 4. Elmhurst, IL.

McKay, Leonard, and Nestor (Wally) Wahlberg. *A Postcard History of San Jose*. San Jose, CA: Memorabilia of San Jose, 1992.

Tillmany, Jack, and Jennifer Dowling. *Theatres of Oakland*. San Francisco, CA: Arcadia Publishing, 2006.

Tillmany, Jack. *Theatres of San Francisco*. San Francisco, CA: Arcadia Publishing, 2005.

ACROSS AMERICA, PEOPLE ARE DISCOVERING SOMETHING WONDERFUL. THEIR HERITAGE.

Arcadia Publishing is the leading local history publisher in the United States. With more than 5,000 titles in print and hundreds of new titles released every year, Arcadia has extensive specialized experience chronicling the history of communities and celebrating America's hidden stories, bringing to life the people, places, and events from the past. To discover the history of other communities across the nation, please visit:

www.arcadiapublishing.com

Customized search tools allow you to find regional history books about the town where you grew up, the cities where your friends and family live, the town where your parents met, or even that retirement spot you've been dreaming about.